I am the Lorax. I speak for the trees.

—from *The Lorax*

The editors would like to thank
ALICE WONDRAK BIEL, PhD,
for assistance in the preparation of this book.

Random House Books for Young Readers
An imprint of Random House Children's Books
A division of Penguin Random House LLC
1745 Broadway, New York, NY 10019
penguinrandomhouse.com
Seussville.com
rhcbooks.com

Library of Congress Cataloging-in-Publication Data is available upon request.
ISBN 979-8-217-22474-6 (trade)

Manufactured in China
10 9 8 7 6 5 4 3 2 1

The authorized representative in the EU for product safety and compliance is Penguin Random House Ireland, Morrison Chambers, 32 Nassau Street, Dublin D02 YH68, Ireland, https://eu-contact.penguin.ie.

Random House Children's Books supports the First Amendment and celebrates the right to read.

Explore the National Parks with Dr. Seuss's Lorax

by Bonnie Worth

illustrated by Aristides Ruiz

Random House New York

I'm the Lorax, my friends,
with a few choice remarks
about places we know of
as national parks!

From the east to the west,
we've set aside land
to preserve nature's treasures,
as I understand.

Like clean water, fresh air,
wild animals, and—I'll say—
spots to view nature
and enjoy outdoor play!

Did you know?

Native, or Indigenous, people originally occupied all these lands and have a deep connection to every national park.

United States
NATIONAL PARKS

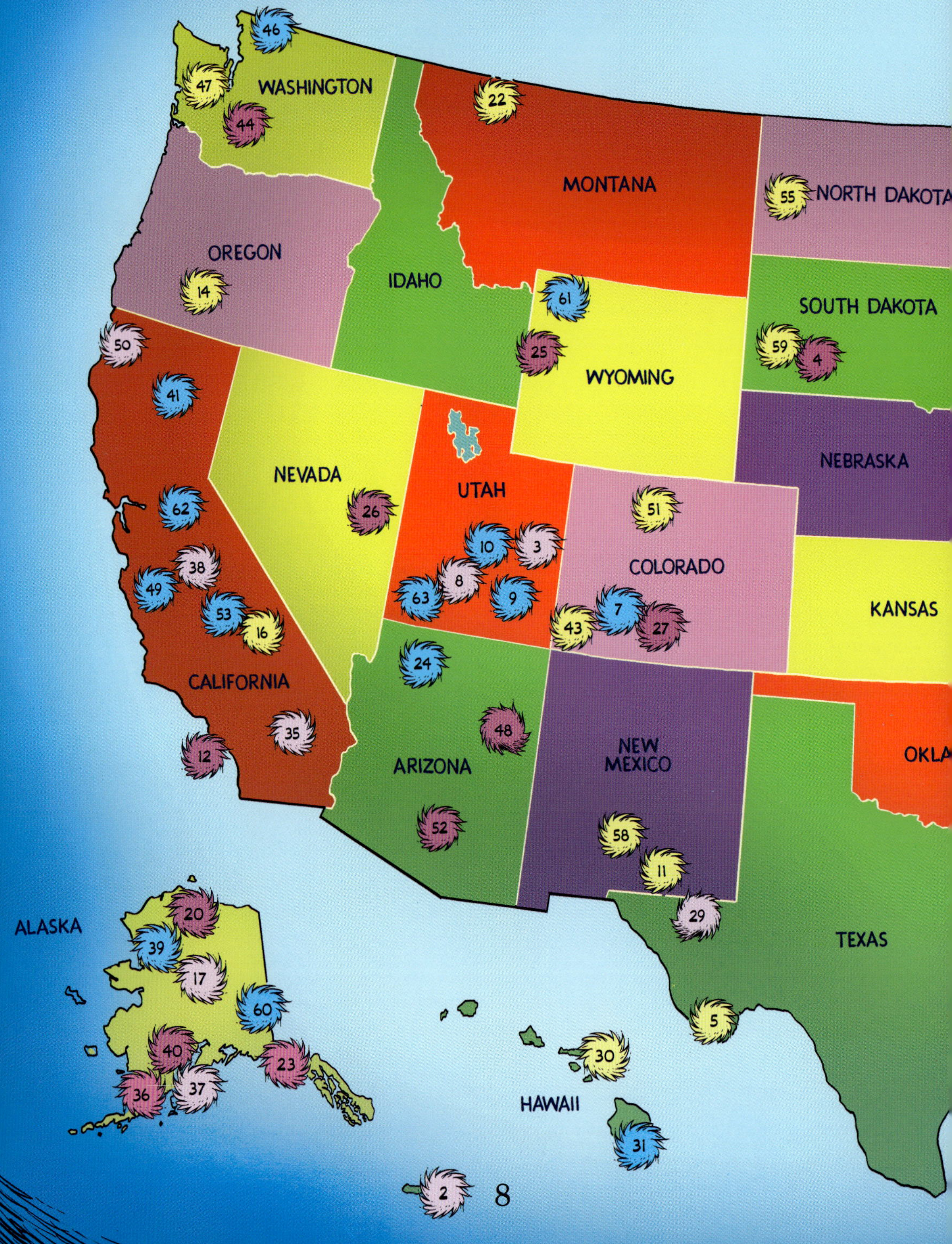

Parks offer such wonders!
We'll tour some of these—
from high peaks to deep canyons
to towering trees.

Turn to page 42 for park names.

Yellowstone National Park

Way out west in Wyoming
is where you will find
a park bigger than Delaware
and Rhode Island combined.

This park is what's called
a volcanic hot spot.
It has hot springs and geysers
that erupt quite a lot.

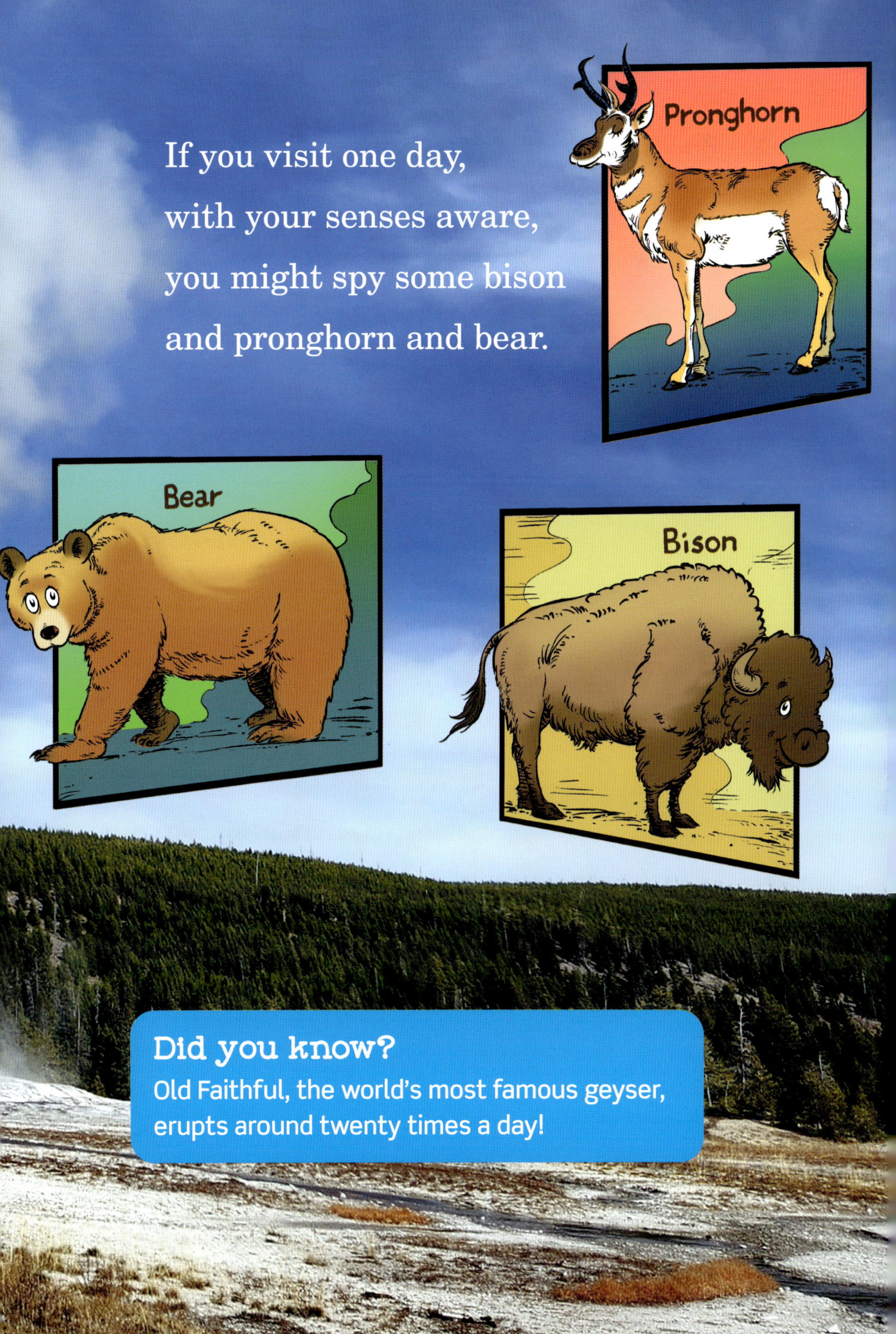

If you visit one day,
with your senses aware,
you might spy some bison
and pronghorn and bear.

Did you know?
Old Faithful, the world's most famous geyser, erupts around twenty times a day!

Did you know?

If the giant sequoia can survive threats like fire, wind, and soil erosion, it can live as long as 3,000 years.

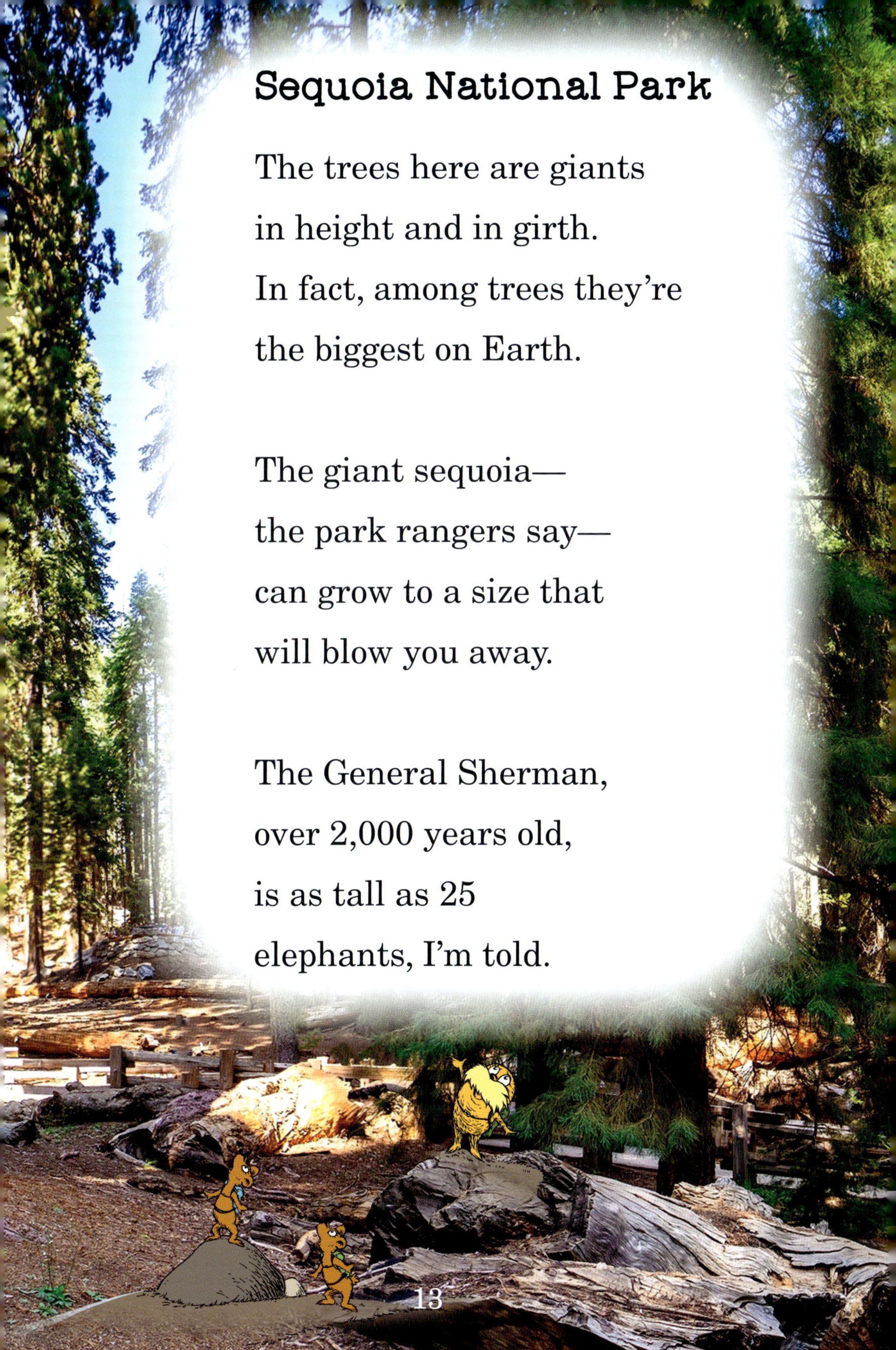

Sequoia National Park

The trees here are giants
in height and in girth.
In fact, among trees they're
the biggest on Earth.

The giant sequoia—
the park rangers say—
can grow to a size that
will blow you away.

The General Sherman,
over 2,000 years old,
is as tall as 25
elephants, I'm told.

Everglades National Park

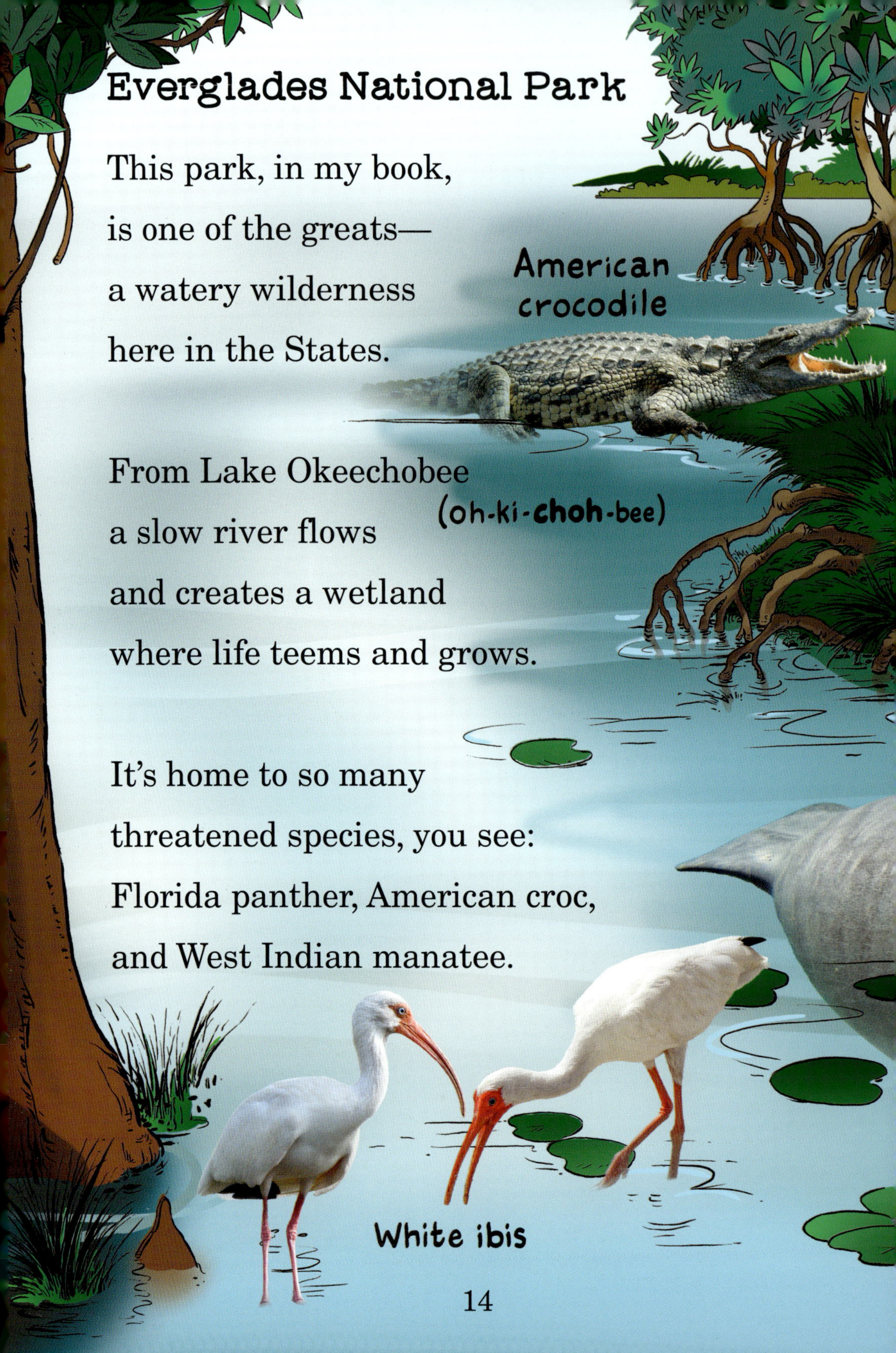

This park, in my book,
is one of the greats—
a watery wilderness
here in the States.

From Lake Okeechobee
a slow river flows
and creates a wetland
where life teems and grows.

It's home to so many
threatened species, you see:
Florida panther, American croc,
and West Indian manatee.

Mangrove forests here
offer shelter—the best!—
for wading birds like
the white ibis to nest.

Death Valley National Park

This valley is not all
that deadly, it seems,
hosting so many species
that can stand its extremes.

In 1913—
I'm not pulling your leg—
it was hot enough here
to fry up an egg.

Denali National Park and Preserve

What's the highest high spot
in the U.S., I ask ya?
It's Denali—a mountain
way up in Alaska!

Great Denali rises
up high in the sky.
Just how high up is it?
About four miles high!

Petrified Forest National Park

This park is a fossilized
forest, you know,
of trees that grew over
215 million years ago.

Who cut these stone logs?
you might want to say.
But nobody did!
They just crack this way!

Did you know?

Petroglyphs are rock carvings made with a stone chisel. The park's Newspaper Rock has over 650 petroglyphs created between 650 and 2,000 years ago.

Joshua Tree National Park

Could this be a Truffula
Tree next to me?
No, it's an agave,
a Joshua tree.

Its strong branches cradle
birds' nests to perfection.
Its spiny leaves offer
small mammals protection.

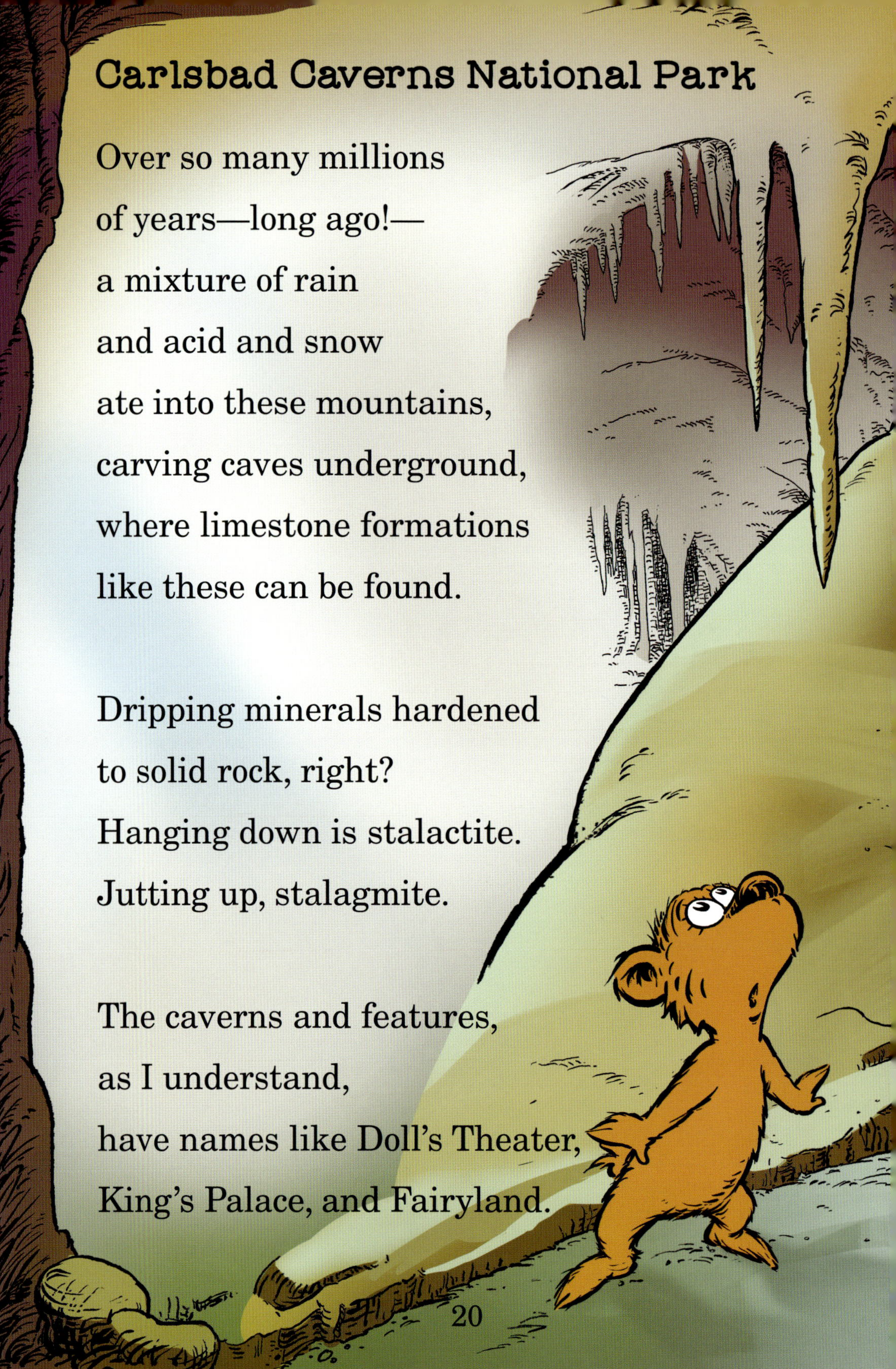

Carlsbad Caverns National Park

Over so many millions
of years—long ago!—
a mixture of rain
and acid and snow
ate into these mountains,
carving caves underground,
where limestone formations
like these can be found.

Dripping minerals hardened
to solid rock, right?
Hanging down is stalactite.
Jutting up, stalagmite.

The caverns and features,
as I understand,
have names like Doll's Theater,
King's Palace, and Fairyland.

King's Palace

Doll's Theater

Great Sand Dunes National Park

These vast, sweeping dunes
are not at the shore.
You'll find them inland.
Let's learn a bit more.

Did you know?
Humans occupied this area as long as 11,000 years ago!

Mountain silt, washed down
in ages long past,
piled up and created
these sand dunes so vast.

Bryce Canyon National Park

While we call this a canyon,
that's not really true.
It's an amphitheater—
a big word for you!

There are hoodoos found here,
as they're commonly known—
tower formations
that are made out of stone.

An amphitheater,
in ancient Greek days,
was where people went
to watch games and plays.

Great Smoky Mountains National Park

Visitors come here
by the millions. I'd say
it's the busiest park
in the whole U.S.A.

The Appalachian Trail,
likely as not,
is one reason this park's
such a popular spot.

Did you know?
The Appalachian Trail stretches over 2,000 miles from Springer Mountain, Georgia, to Mount Katahdin in Maine.

Acadia National Park

On Maine's rocky coast,
you might spot a bear,
a harbor seal—or even
a moose here and there.

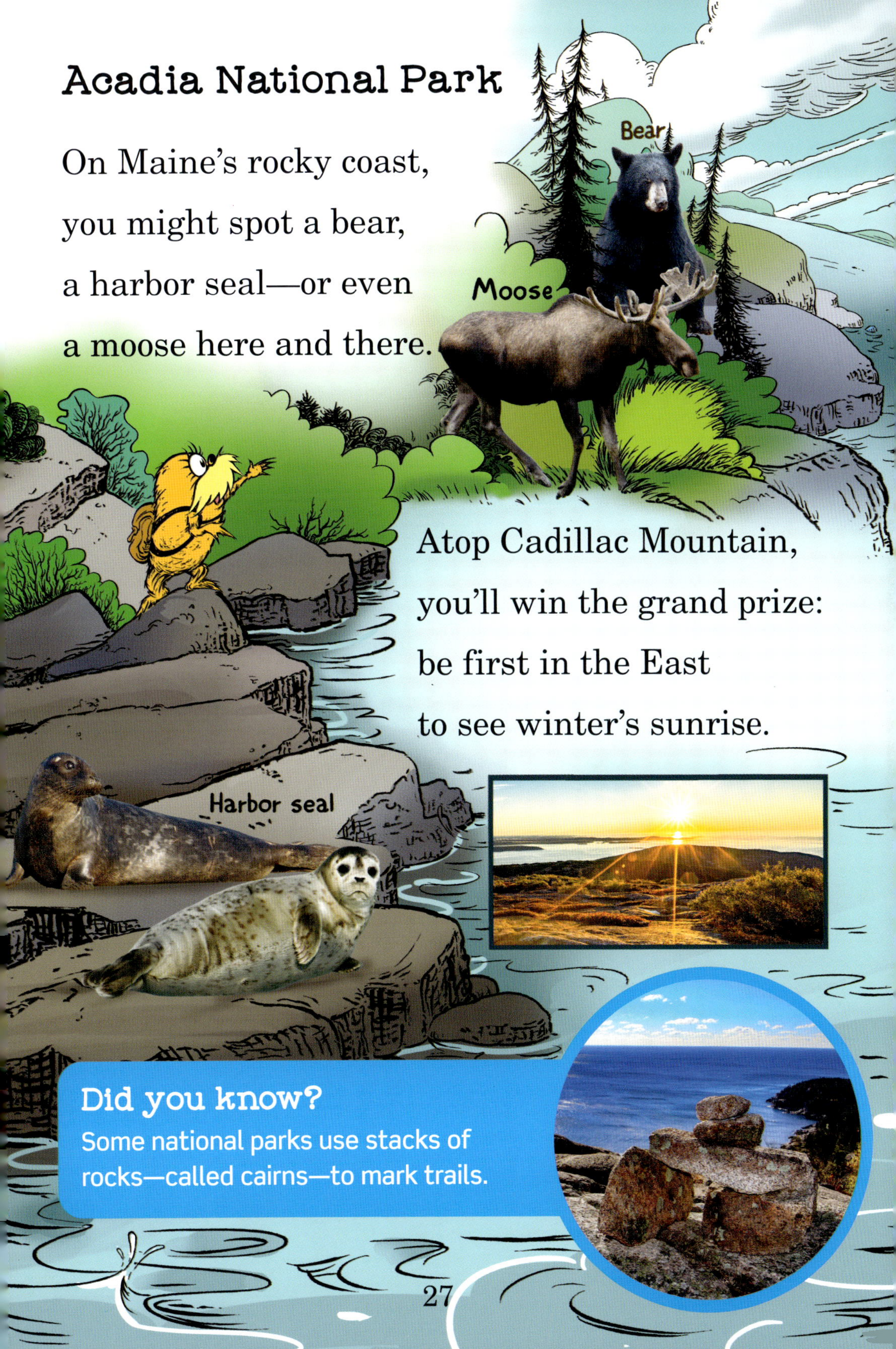

Atop Cadillac Mountain,
you'll win the grand prize:
be first in the East
to see winter's sunrise.

Did you know?
Some national parks use stacks of rocks—called cairns—to mark trails.

Badlands National Park

Stark, rocky, and arid!
The Lakota people had
a name for this place—
and it was Land Bad.

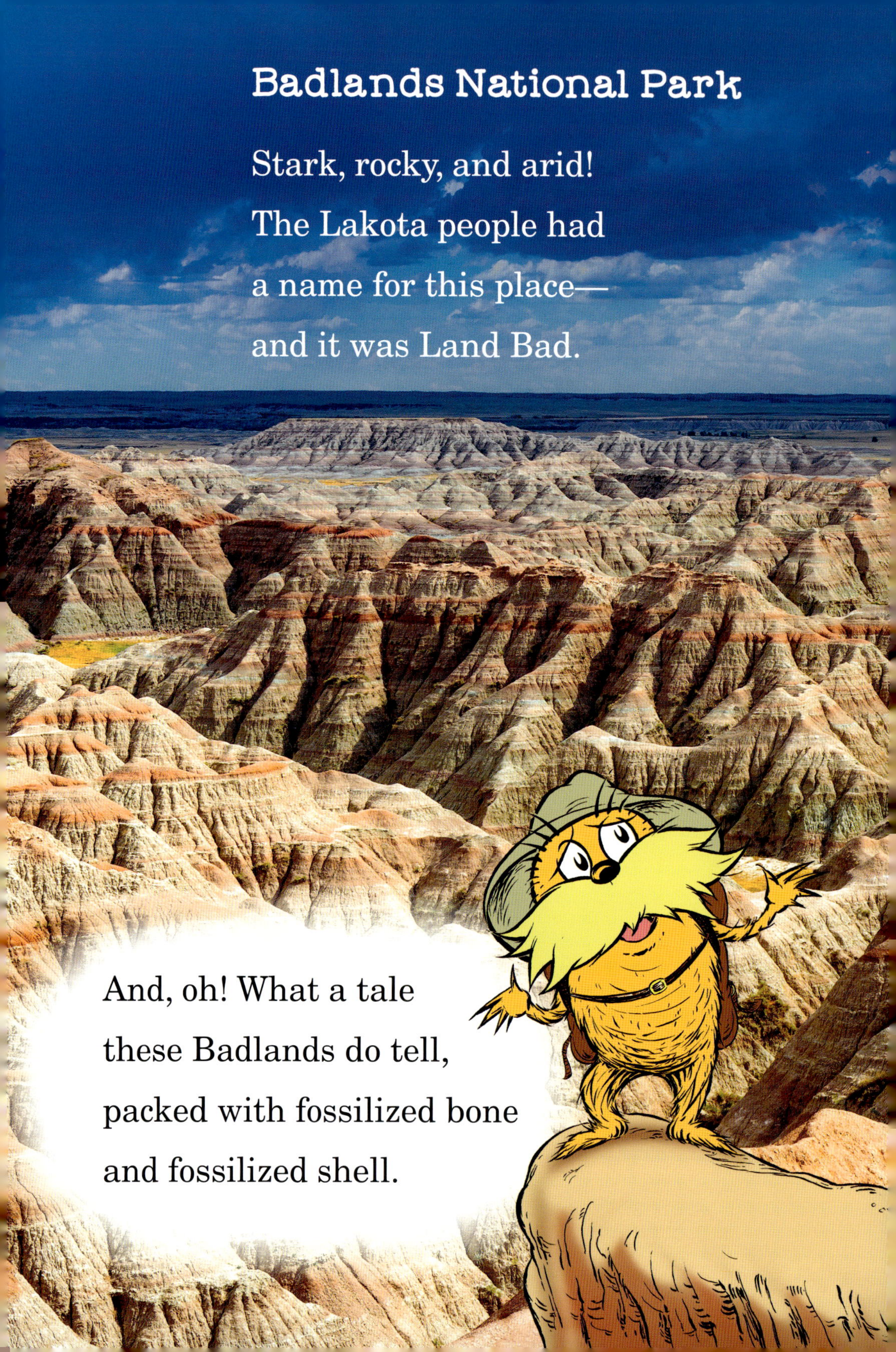

And, oh! What a tale
these Badlands do tell,
packed with fossilized bone
and fossilized shell.

Scientists have found,
on their many digs,
the ancestors of rhinos,
sheep, horses, and pigs.

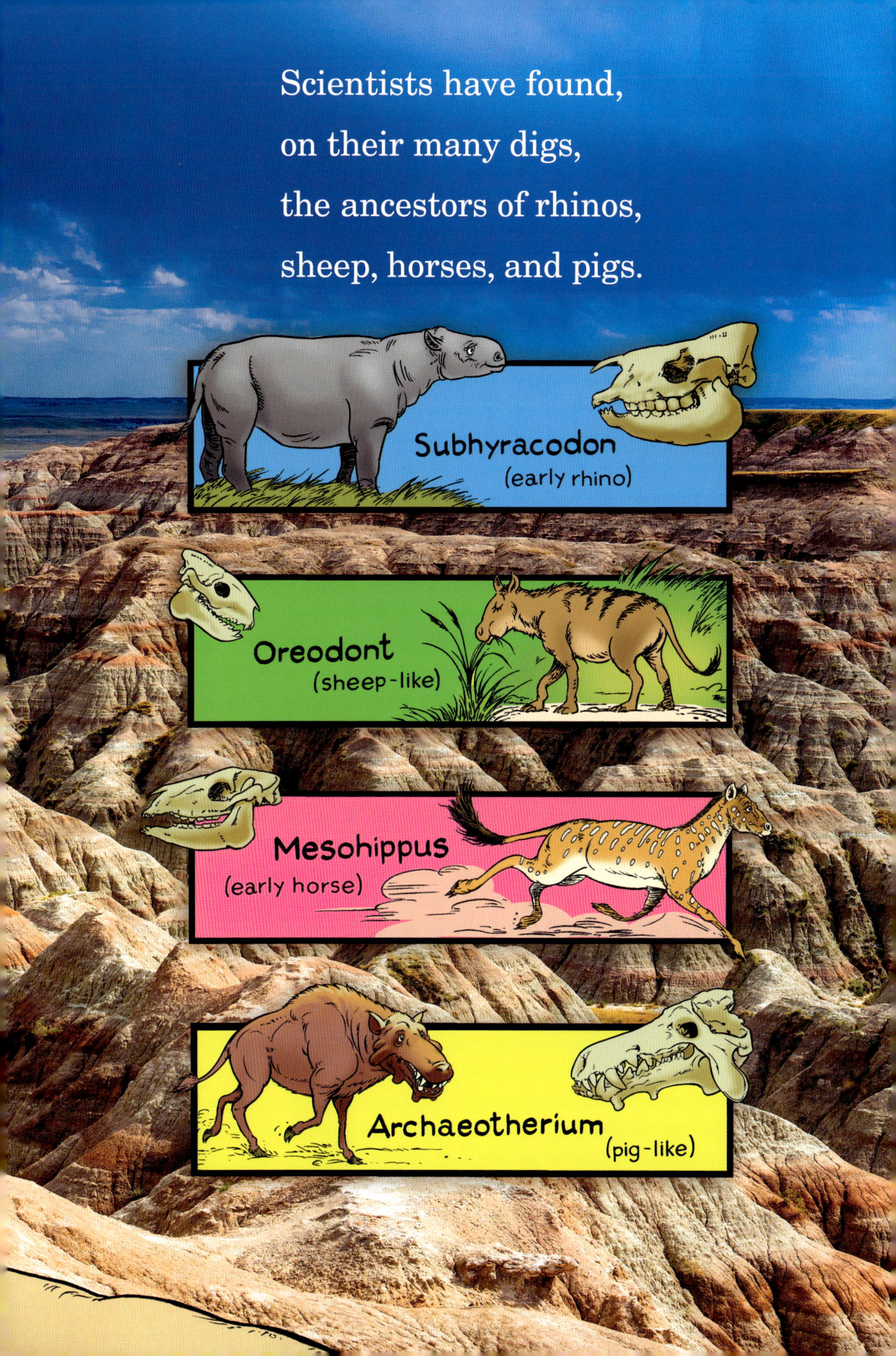

Hawai‘i Volcanoes National Park

The island of Hawai‘i,
where folks say aloha,
is the home of volcanoes—
Kīlauea and Maunaloa.

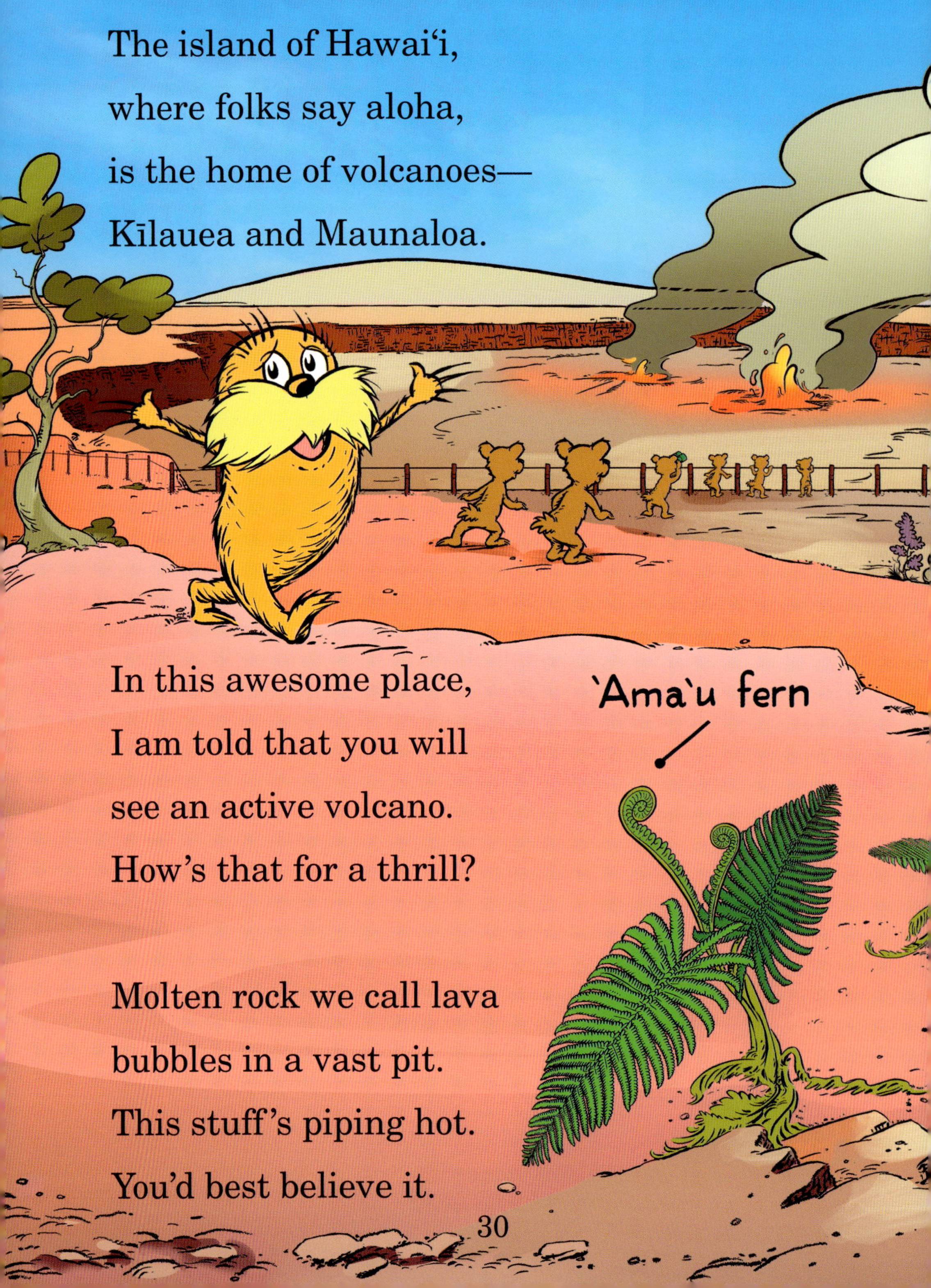

In this awesome place,
I am told that you will
see an active volcano.
How's that for a thrill?

Molten rock we call lava
bubbles in a vast pit.
This stuff's piping hot.
You'd best believe it.

This park is a place
of incomparable worth.
There are plants and birds
like no place on Earth.
ʻŌhiʻa lehua
ʻApapane
ʻAmakihi

Grand Canyon National Park

Are you ready for nature's
most eye-popping show?
Stand right next to me
on the Colorado Plateau.

The Colorado River
wore a gorge—a wide rut—
through layers of rock.
It made a deep cut.

The layers are colored
so brightly, some say,
you'll thrill to the sight
of this awesome display.

Hiking trails lead down
to the river below.
They are steep and narrow.
The going is slow.

But if you are feeling
daring one day—
climb onto a mule and
ride down the whole way!

Did you know?
The Grand Canyon is so deep that its weather varies dramatically. When it's freezing and rainy up on the North Rim, it might be hot and dry down at Phantom Ranch.

Visit the Parks!

There are so many parks.
We have seen just a few.
Want to visit a park?
Here are some things you should do:

On the day of your visit,
make sure that you pack
water, maps, sunscreen,
and a good salty snack.

Bring first-aid supplies,
extra clothes or a jacket.
The weather can change.
You'll be glad that you packed it!

Bring a notebook and camera
because you might like
to keep track of the sights
that you see on your hike.

Did you know?

In addition to national parks, there are lots of other National Park Service sites you can visit, including monuments, seashores, and historic places!

Go on a Virtual Visit!

You can't always jump
in a train, plane, or car
and travel to places
where national parks are.

But hop on a computer
and soon you can be
on a virtual park tour.
Oh, the things you will see!

I speak for all nature
and say this to you:
Our national parks
could use YOUR help, too.

Stick to the trails
and do not ever litter.
Look but don't touch
each plant and each critter.

Learn all about them—
and then you will see
we are all of us part
of Earth's big family.

Resources to Check Out

The **National Park Service** offers a variety of excellent online resources. Check out **Kids in Parks** and learn how to become a Junior Ranger—online or at a national park! Also available are downloadable activity books, virtual tours, and games. Visit nps.gov/kids/index.htm. Educators looking for classroom activities and lesson plans for students can visit nps.gov/teachers/index.htm.

To learn more about Indigenous Americans' connection to specific national parks, visit nps.gov/subjects/americanindians/index.htm.

The **National Park Foundation** is the nonprofit partner of the National Park Service. Visit the **Parks at Home** section of the foundation's website for virtual tours, activities, games, printouts, and more! nationalparks.org/theme/parks-at-home

National parks shown on pages 8–9:

1. Acadia
2. American Samoa
3. Arches
4. Badlands
5. Big Bend
6. Biscayne
7. Black Canyon of the Gunnison
8. Bryce Canyon
9. Canyonlands
10. Capitol Reef
11. Carlsbad Caverns
12. Channel Islands
13. Congaree
14. Crater Lake
15. Cuyahoga Valley
16. Death Valley
17. Denali
18. Dry Tortugas
19. Everglades
20. Gates of the Arctic
21. Gateway Arch
22. Glacier
23. Glacier Bay
24. Grand Canyon
25. Grand Teton
26. Great Basin
27. Great Sand Dunes
28. Great Smoky Mountains
29. Guadalupe Mountains
30. Haleakalā
31. Hawai'i Volcanoes
32. Hot Springs
33. Indiana Dunes
34. Isle Royale
35. Joshua Tree
36. Katmai
37. Kenai Fjords
38. Kings Canyon
39. Kobuk Valley
40. Lake Clark
41. Lassen Volcanic
42. Mammoth Cave
43. Mesa Verde
44. Mount Rainier
45. New River Gorge
46. North Cascades
47. Olympic
48. Petrified Forest
49. Pinnacles
50. Redwood
51. Rocky Mountain
52. Saguaro
53. Sequoia
54. Shenandoah
55. Theodore Roosevelt
56. Virgin Islands
57. Voyageurs
58. White Sands
59. Wind Cave
60. Wrangell–St. Elias
61. Yellowstone
62. Yosemite
63. Zion

Glossary

Amphitheater: An open-ended, round structure, either natural or human-made.

Cavern: A cave or room in a cave.

Features: Special attractions.

Formation: A kind of rock that stands as a single unit.

Fossil: The remains, or the impression of remains, of a prehistoric creature or plant.

Geyser: A boiling hot spring that sends steam and water shooting into the air.

Girth: The measurement around the outside of something.

Gorge: A narrow, deep valley with steep sides, usually with a stream running through it.

Indigenous: Originally in or native to a given place.

Plateau: An area of level, high ground.

Stalactite: A mineral formation caused by dripping water that hangs like an icicle from the roof of a cave.

Stalagmite: A mineral formation caused by dripping water that rises from the floor of a cave.

Virtual: A lifelike experience created by computer software.

Index

The LORAX
Dr. Seuss

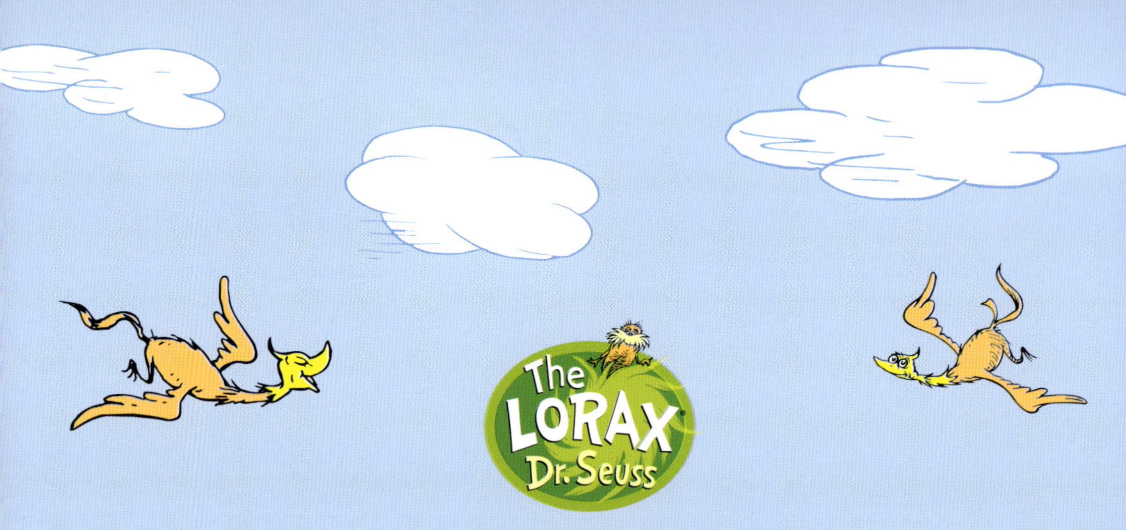

Encourage a love of nature
and respect for the environment in children of ALL ages
with these books featuring Dr. Seuss's Lorax!

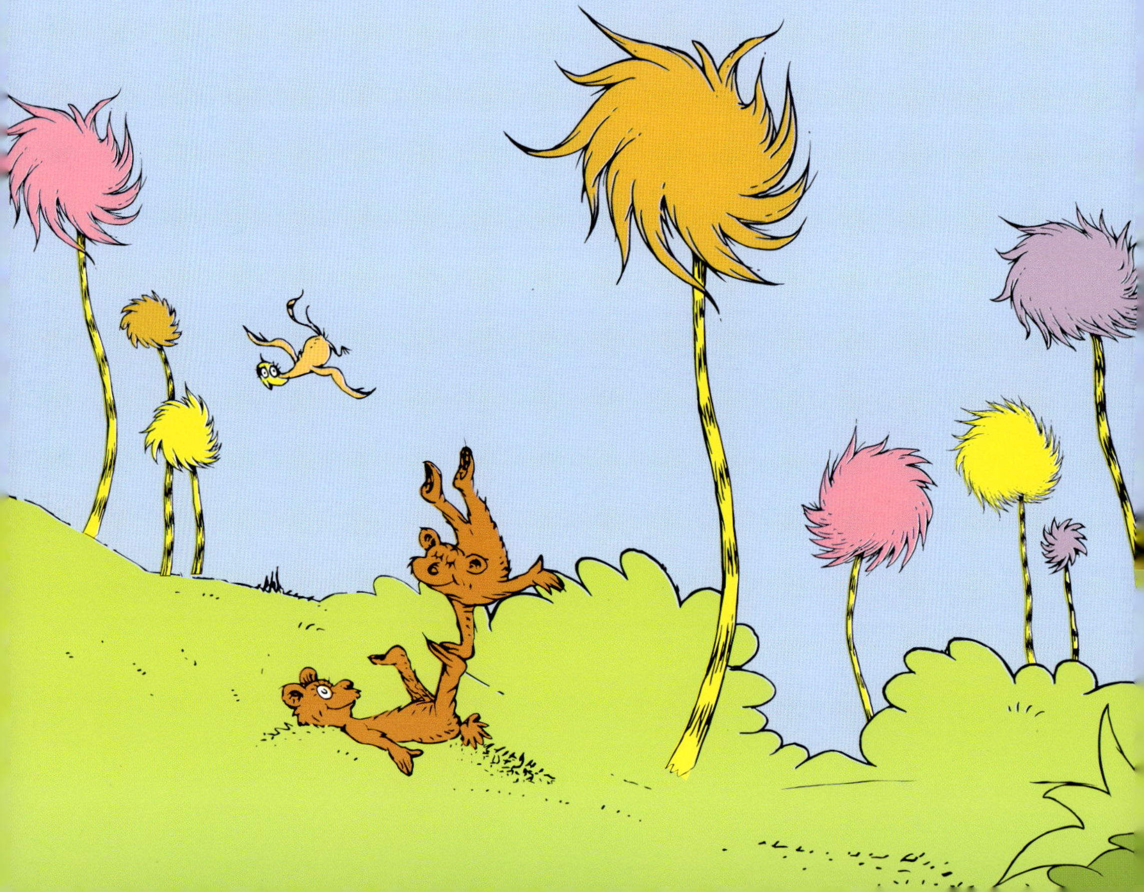